EARTHWISE
Getting Around

Jim Pipe

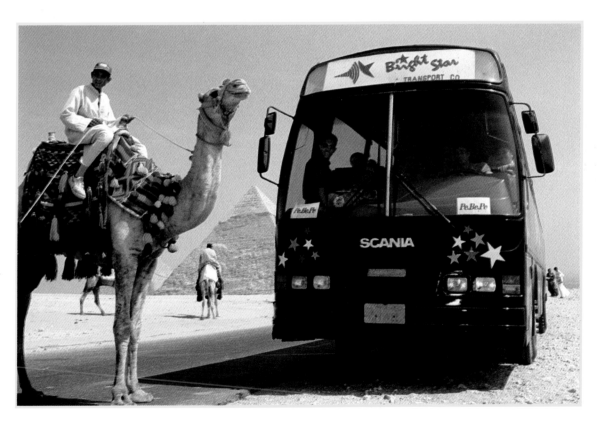

Franklin Watts
London • Sydney

CONTENTS

© Aladdin Books Ltd 2004

Designed and produced by
Aladdin Books Ltd
28 Percy Street
London W1T 2BZ

First published in
Great Britain in 2004 by
Franklin Watts
96 Leonard Street
London EC2A 4XD

Editor
Katie Harker

Educational Consultant
Jackie Holderness

Series Design
Flick, Book Design and
Graphics

Designer
Simon Morse

Picture Research
Brian Hunter Smart

ISBN 0 7496 5499 6

A catalogue record for this
book is available from the
British Library.

Printed in UAE

INTRODUCTION

Most of us make several journeys each day. We may walk to school, take the bus to the shops, or travel in a car to visit friends. Maps and routes help us to find our way. Sometimes, we make longer journeys using planes and trains. There are lots of different ways to get around!

HOW TO USE THIS BOOK

Look for the symbol of the magnifying glass for tips and ideas on what to look for where you live.

The paintbrush boxes contain activities that may relate to transport in your local area.

JOURNEYS

How many journeys do you make in a week? Like many people today, you may move around a lot. Most towns are growing, so people live further and further from where they work or go to school. Families use buses or cars to go shopping. Travel has also become less expensive. Many people now fly long distances to go on holiday.

Where Do You Go?

School bus

Walking to the shops

Think about the different journeys your family makes:

- Shopping – to get things you need
- Daily travel – to get to school or work
- Special journeys – to visit family and friends, to go on holiday, to move house
- Emergencies – to go to hospital

Write down how you would travel. When would you fly in a plane and when would you cycle?

Traffic is a word used to describe vehicles on the move, such as cars, bicycles, motor rickshaws (left) and buses.

When lots of people travel at the same time, it can cause traffic jams. If there are too many vehicles, everyone has to move very slowly.

TRANSPORT

Any vehicle that helps to move people or goods is a type of transport. What vehicles can you see in your area? As well as cars and buses, perhaps some people still use animals to pull carts or sleds. If you live near a lake or the sea, look out for boats. Don't forget to look up for aeroplanes in the sky!

Dog sled

Boat

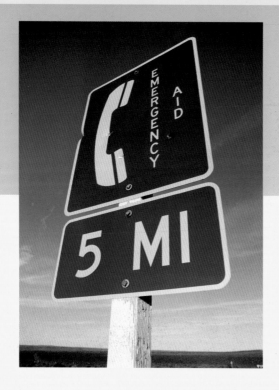

Most routes have signs that tell us which way to go and how far away places are. They help us to work out how long a journey will take.

ROUTES

You may be going to the shops or flying off on holiday, but every journey you take follows a route. Paths, pavements, streets, roads and rivers all provide routes for us to follow.

Routes are important because when we set out on a journey we usually can't see the place we want to reach.

O N • THE • LEVEL

It is much easier to travel along a flat path than it is to climb up and down hills. That is why viaducts and cuttings are used to create a level route for cars or trains.

A viaduct is a bridge that crosses a valley (right). Cuttings are where hills have been cut away. Can you spot any in your area?

The best route is not always the quickest or shortest. When you are holiday, for instance, you might take a route that has beautiful scenery. This is more relaxing than rushing along a motorway where there is little to see.

The shortest route between two places is a straight line. We call this a direct route. However, hills, buildings, lakes, or the sea can get in the way. This forces the route to twist and bend. But tunnels and bridges can help a road to keep going in a straight line.

Route Race

Set a route for your friends across school. See who can find the quickest route. Use a watch to time them. Then draw a map to show their different routes. Did the quickest route follow a straight line?

LANDMARKS

On short journeys, we can remember the route by looking for landmarks. These are objects on the landscape that are easily spotted. Landmarks can be natural features, such as cliffs, lakes and woods. Landmarks can also be tall buildings, such as churches or mosque towers. Even when we have a map, landmarks are helpful because they give us clues about where we are.

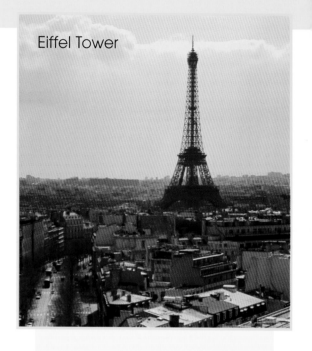
Eiffel Tower

Many cities have a particularly tall landmark that can be seen from far away. In Paris, you can see the Eiffel Tower for many miles. In San Francisco, the Golden Gate bridge looms high over the harbour entrance.

Tall buildings make good landmarks.

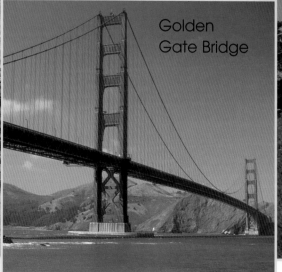
Golden Gate Bridge

Route Map

Think about a short journey that you know well, such as the route to a friend's house or your route to school. Make a list of landmarks you pass. You may want to draw your journey, like this example (right). Remember to show landmarks and the places where you turn left or right, or where you have to cross the road.

These maps show the same place.

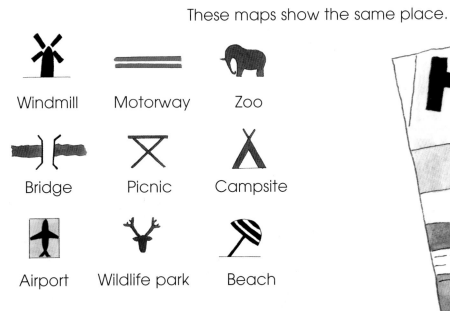

Windmill	Motorway	Zoo
Bridge	Picnic	Campsite
Airport	Wildlife park	Beach

Compare your route map with a street map of the same area. Street maps show landmarks, such as bridges and beaches, using symbols (above). On most maps there is a list or "key" telling you what these symbols mean.

MAPS

Maps help us to find our way around unfamiliar places. Street maps show roads and buildings in a town. Walking maps show features such as hills, woods and rivers. A tourist map points out interesting places to visit. World maps show all the continents, islands and oceans of the world.

Route maps such as a road atlas help us to plan journeys. Important roads look the biggest.

COMPASS

Wherever you are, a compass can tell you in which direction you are going. Line up the needle so that it is pointing to N for north. With the needle in this position, the letters E, S and W point to east, south and west. Using a compass and map together makes it easy to know exactly where you are!

Most modern maps are based on photographs taken from the air. A plane flies over the area and a camera takes photographs of the ground below.

The photos are put together to give the map-maker a view of the whole area. Today, maps are also made from pictures taken by satellites in space (main picture).

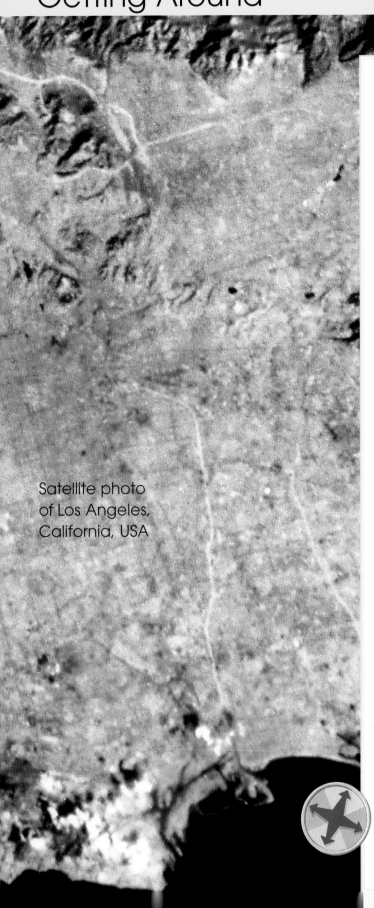

Satellite photo
of Los Angeles,
California, USA

Walking Map

Walking maps show natural features such as cliffs as well as man-made paths, roads and buildings. Lines called contours show the height of the land. Where the lines are close together, the hill is steep. Next time you go for a walk in the country, use a map to follow your route. Look out for features such as rivers that can help you to find your way.

Wood   Contour lines   Railway cutting

HOW DO I GET THERE?

Using maps, we can plan our route. Then we can decide how we want to travel. Today, there are lots of different ways of getting around.

On short journeys you might walk, cycle or take the bus. On longer journeys you might travel in a car or train, fly from an airport, or take a ferry.

Paint Your Journey

Hydrofoil

Many artists like to paint transport, such as ships or planes. Others like to paint the countryside when they travel. Paint your own picture of your favourite transport or a scene from a journey you know well.

Drawing lines behind a plane shows that it is moving!

Road

Motor vehicles such as cars, buses and motorbikes are a handy way to get around. They can pick you up from your front door!

Rail

Fast trains link large towns. Slower trains link places on the edge of a city, called suburbs, with the city centre. A train can carry the same number of passengers as 1,000 cars.

Air

Planes are the fastest way to travel. Many jetliners travel at around 900 km/h. They can carry 500 people across the Atlantic Ocean in 5 hours.

Sea

Ships cross oceans, providing links between continents. Ferries can carry 1,000 passengers and 400 cars across seas and lakes. Some have cabins for people to sleep in on long journeys.

A plane carries a parcel across the world.

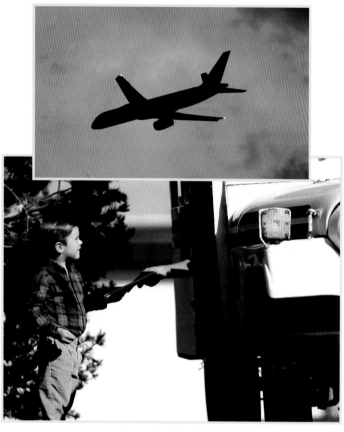

A van brings it to your door!

MOVING GOODS

Transport also helps us to move heavy goods from one place to another. Factories need materials which come from different places around the world. A lot of the food that we eat is grown in other countries. Planes are used for small or urgent deliveries. Lorries, trains and ships are better for moving heavy loads.

Be a Lorry Driver

Write a story about what it is like to be a lorry driver. First, you might pick up a container from a ship. Lorries can carry goods a long way, so you may drive for many hours. You can talk to other drivers using a two-way radio. In a big lorry, you may even sleep in a bed at the back of the cab!

Container ship

Lorry

The journey from an oil field to a petrol pump

After oil is pumped out of the ground, it travels along huge **pipelines** for part of its journey. The Trans-Alaska Pipeline crosses three mountain ranges and 300 rivers!

Ships, called **tankers**, transport the oil on water. The largest tankers can hold more than a million barrels of oil. Barges carry the oil on rivers.

The oil is pumped from the ship to a refinery, where the oil is made into petrol for cars. Then big **lorries** carry the petrol to service stations.

When we go to a petrol or service station, the petrol is pumped into our car's **petrol tank** along a pipe. The oil has come a very long way!

Trains can carry goods over very long distances. The world's longest railway line is in Russia. It is 9,000 kilometres long!

Trains may pull around 2,500 tonnes of coal, wood or building materials, the same amount as 100 big lorries. But because trains run on tracks, they cannot provide a door-to-door service.

LOCAL TRANSPORT

How do people move around in your area? In most parts of the world, people use buses on short journeys. Many big cities also have a rail network, either above or under the ground. Trains link city centres with areas further out, called "suburbs". In less developed regions, people use animals, such as horses and donkeys, to move goods about.

Tram

Underground train

In large cities, buses carry thousands of people each day. At a bus stop you can use a timetable to find out where a bus goes, when it will arrive, and how long the journey will take.

Network maps help us to find our way around cities. Different colours show different routes. Using the map below, work out how to get from Greenfields to Cow Lane in the fewest stops.

Greenfields

Rail Station

Bus Station

Oak Road   Riverside

Old Market

Stable Street

Temple Street

White Cross

Cow Lane

South Station

To the Airport

Line 1

Line 2

Line 3

Interchange: where two lines meet, links with other transport networks

C YCLE • PATHS

In many towns there are routes for bicycles, called cycle paths. Look out for cycle paths near you. They are marked by signs (below) or may be coloured red or green.

Cycle lanes often keep cyclists away from busy car routes. They make cycling safer. But wherever you are cycling you should always wear a helmet and bright clothing.

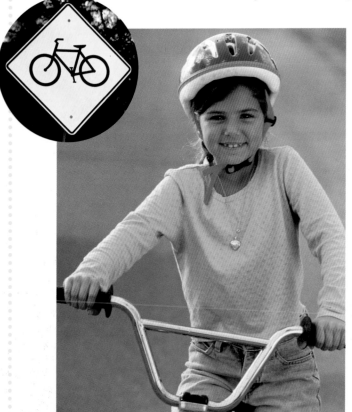

USING NETWORKS

Today, everyone relies on good transport links to deliver food and other goods to shops. Many people travel long distances to do business or go on holiday. Most types of transport are linked by global (worldwide) networks. A network means lots of routes linked to each other.

Many parts of the world are linked by a system of long, fast roads, called highways or motorways (right).

The longest road system in the world is the Pan-American Highway. This connects the capitals of 17 countries in South America and is over 47,000 kilometres long!

For thousands of years, travelling by road was slow, dangerous and uncomfortable. When railway networks were built 150 years ago, it suddenly became much easier to move about on land. Since aeroplanes were invented in 1903, flying has become a popular form of transport.

Today, 500 million people a year travel around the world by air.

Local network – bus/tram

Rail network

Air network

Sea network

How Networks Connect

On long journeys, people often use local networks that connect with bigger networks. For instance, you might take a bus to your nearest train station, then catch a train to the airport. If you look at a timetable for each part of the journey, you can make sure that you have plenty of time to make your connections.

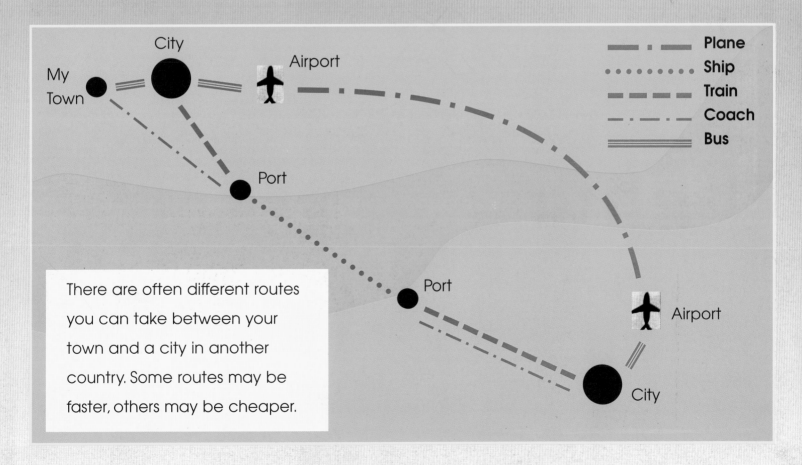

City

Airport

My Town

Port

Plane
Ship
Train
Coach
Bus

Port

Airport

City

There are often different routes you can take between your town and a city in another country. Some routes may be faster, others may be cheaper.

Ship ties up at port

MAKING IT WORK

Each transport network needs different things to make it work. Cars and lorries need good smooth roads and places to fill up with fuel. Trains need smooth tracks and railway stations where people can get on and off. Planes need airports to take off and land. Ships need harbours where they can tie up and unload.

Passengers need to be looked after, too. Motorway service stations and ships have special areas for eating (right), toilets, shops and play areas for children. On trains,

coaches and aeroplanes there is less room so people usually sit in one place. Staff serve food and drinks from trolleys.

Like cars and ships, planes need to fill up with fuel before a long journey. The fuel is pumped into tanks under the wings.

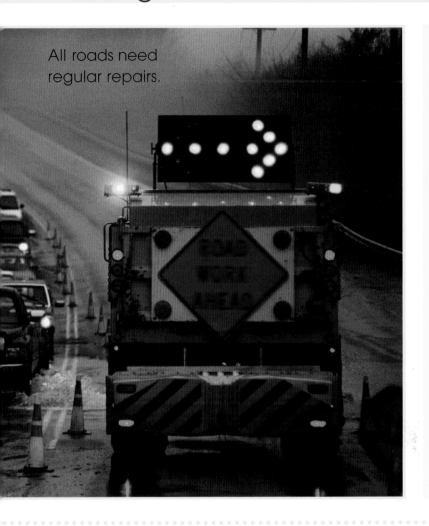

All roads need regular repairs.

All vehicles need help to avoid other vehicles or potential hazards. Tugs help big ships to steer in narrow rivers and harbours.

Traffic lights and lanes help vehicles to avoid each other where two roads meet. Lights also tell train drivers when to wait for trains coming from the other direction.

AIRPORT • JOBS

If you visit an airport, watch out for all the different people at work in shops, customs or passport control, at ticket desks, or looking after the planes. Try to spot the control tower. Here, air traffic controllers (right) let pilots know when it is their turn to take off or land.

TRANSPORT PROBLEMS

Bigger, faster transport networks help us to move around more easily. But every type of transport can cause problems. For example, cars are very convenient. They take us exactly where we want to go. However, cars also create lots of noise and pollution. They also use large amounts of petrol and oil and are expensive to make. The roads they use cut through the countryside (above), destroying natural habitats.

There are 400 million cars in the world today. The amount of traffic in towns and cities all over the world is growing rapidly. Although a lot of money is being spent on new roads, there are still traffic jams in many places.

NOISE • POLLUTION

Cars, trains and planes can make a lot of noise. As a result, living near an airport, a busy road or a railway line can be very annoying!

Smog is a mixture of smoke and fog. It makes the air look hazy. Smog is caused by fumes from cars and factories. In large cities, such as Athens and Los Angeles (below), smog is a big problem in the summer months.

All over the world, cars and lorries are damaging the environment. The fumes from vehicles can lead to health problems, such as asthma and cancer. Fumes also build up in the atmosphere. They mix with water in the air, causing acid rain. When it falls, this damages trees and other plants. Jet planes also harm the environment. Because they fly so high, their fumes go straight into the atmosphere.

The weather can cause problems for vehicles. In autumn, leaves on railway lines can slow down trains. Fog and snow (above) can make driving dangerous. Storms can make travel dangerous for cars, planes and ships.

MOVING FORWARDS

Towns and cities are dealing with local transport problems in different ways. Many cities encourage drivers to travel into the centre by bus or train. In some towns, cars must give way to pedestrians and the streets are safer for children. Other cities use tram lines to make travel easier in the city centre.

Traffic Schemes

There is no easy answer to traffic problems. For example, if you make roads better, they attract more cars! But traffic schemes can keep cars and lorries out of the city centre. This can make it safer for pedestrians and will reduce pollution.

Tram System

Amsterdam, Hong Kong and Dublin all have a tram system that helps to reduce traffic in the city centre.

TRAFFIC • SURVEY

Study the traffic in your area with a friend and an adult. Which are the noisiest or busiest roads? Do heavy lorries create lots of fumes? Are there places where children can cross the road safely?

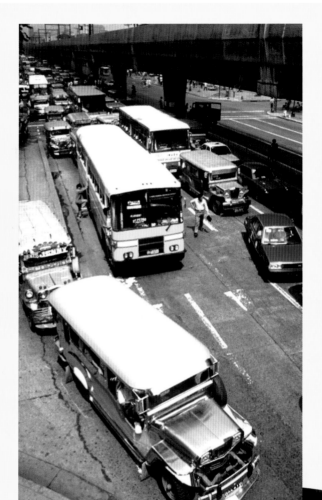

Park and Ride

In some cities, drivers are encouraged to park their cars on the edge of the city and travel into town using bus services. Buses often have their own lanes and can travel quickly around town.

Pedestrian Areas

Many town centres have pedestrian areas. These are streets where vehicles cannot go.

Congestion Charge

In London, drivers must pay a congestion charge if they want to drive in the city centre. This aims to encourage drivers to use public transport instead.

When cars park on the side of the street it can make it hard for the traffic to flow quickly. So, in busy streets, there are strict parking rules – you may be fined if you block a route.

Communications are all of the things that we use to keep in touch or pass on information. Communications include radios, TVs, telephones and the internet. Good communications help companies to trade goods and services all over the world.

WORLDWIDE LINKS

People are travelling more and more. Air routes link cities all over the world. But you are linked to the world in lots of other ways, too. You can find out what is happening in other countries from newspapers, the internet or the television. More and more of the things you eat and the items you use come from faraway places.

A big airport links places all over the world.

Journey Search

If you are going on a long journey, such as a holiday, ask your parents or teacher to help you find out about your journey using the internet. You can find where you are going on a map. If you are flying, you can work out what places you will be flying over!

M ADE • IN • CHINA?

Many objects have a label on them showing the country in which they were made. Do a survey of ten objects around your home or classroom. See if you can find out where they come from. Then locate these places on a map of the world or a globe (below).

Journeys of the Future

Space shuttles already take astronauts into space. We also use satellites that circle the Earth, bouncing TV signals or telephone calls to the other side of the world. In the future, there may be networks linking Earth with the Moon or Mars!

HOW CAN WE HELP?

No one likes sitting in a traffic jam for hours. But everyone can help. The simplest way is for people to walk or cycle on short journeys.

On longer journeys it is better to use a bus or train rather than a car. A bus can carry 70 people, but often there are only one or two people in a car. So, using a bus creates less traffic, and less fumes.

R OAD • SAFETY

Car crashes kill 400,000 people around the world each year. Millions of minor accidents damage cars and cause traffic jams. But most accidents can be avoided if drivers follow the rules of the road and drive carefully. You can keep safe by sitting in the rear seat and wearing a seatbelt. On foot, always cross a street at a pedestrian crossing. Look in both directions before walking across.

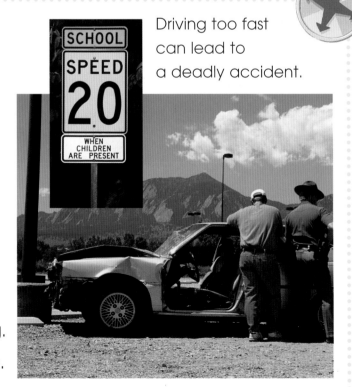

Driving too fast can lead to a deadly accident.

Sharing a car

Taking the bus

Changing Our Ways

Here are some simple ideas for changing your family's travel habits:

- Do you really need to make that journey?
- Use a bicycle for short journeys.
- Walk to school with friends or a parent.
- Your parents can share lifts with other parents to take you and your friends to school.
- Workers can also share lifts to go to work.
- If possible, use a bus rather than a car.
- Avoid the rush hour.

A BIKE is a fun way to travel!

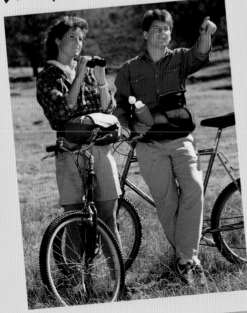

Poster Power

Many people enjoy driving their own cars. But how would you persuade them to change? Design a poster encouraging people to walk or cycle on short journeys, or to use public transport. Mention the advantages. For example, cycling is good for your health and can be very relaxing.

USEFUL WORDS

communications – instruments that we use to exchange information, such as televisions, telephones and the internet.

compass – an instrument used for finding direction, usually with a magnetised needle which points to magnetic north.

continent – one of the Earth's large land masses, such as Africa or Asia.

contour – a line on a map or chart joining points of equal height or depth.

cutting – where hills have been cut away to build a road or railway.

goods – products that are carried, usually by air, rail, land or sea.

interchange – interconnecting roads and bridges designed to prevent streams of traffic crossing one another.

landmark – a prominent or well-known object or feature of a particular landscape.

network – lots of routes linked to each other.

pedestrian – a person travelling on foot.

pollution – harmful or poisonous substances introduced into the environment.

route – the choice of roads used to get to a place.

satellite – a device orbiting the Earth, used to transmit information.

suburb – a residential district situated on the outskirts of a city or town.

traffic – vehicles on the move, such as cars, buses and lorries.

viaduct – a bridge, usually for carrying a road or railway across a valley.

Find Out More

Books: Geography for Fun: People and Places (Franklin Watts), Natural and Environmental Disasters (Franklin Watts).

Websites: www.ecokids.ca
www.howstuffworks.com
www.youngtransnet.org.uk

P AST • TIMES

Look out for older types of transport in your area or when you are on holiday. In some city centres you can still travel by horse and cart. In some towns you can also take a short ride on a steam railway. If you live near a canal, see if you can spot the long canal boats. If you live by the sea, look out for tall sailing ships.

INDEX

Photocredits

Abbreviations: l-left, r-right, b-bottom, t-top, c-centre, m-middle

Front cover tl & br, back cover, 5brt, 6tl, 13tl, 14ml, 15tl, 15mtr, 17c, 21mr, 22tl, 22bl, 22-23, 23b, 25br, 26c, 26br, 27mt, 28tl, 29bl, 30mr — Photodisc. Front cover tr & bl, 2-3, 6br, 7, 8tr, 13tr, 13bl, 14tl, 14br, 16mr, 18 both, 19tl, 19c, 20tl, 20-21t, 21tr, 21br, 22br, 28b, 29mr, 30-31, 31bl — Digital Stock. Front cover inset, 3b, 4mr, 17br, 27mr, 29tr — Brand X Pictures. 1, 16b, 20br — Scania. 4tl, 5t, 19mt, 25tl — Flat Earth. 5brb — Jacquelyn Zettles/USCG. 4br, 12tl, 17tl, 20bm — PBD. 7tl, 15mtl, 16tr, 24br, 25bl, 30bl — Corel. 7br, 10-11, 19ml, 27bl — Corbis. 8bl, 8br — PhotoEssentials. 10c, 10bm, 13br, 24bl — Select Pictures. 14mr — USDA. 15tr — Comstock. 15br — Ken Hammond/USDA. 21bm — Eric A Clement/US Navy. 25tr — Brian Hunter Smart. 26tl — Digital Vision. Special thanks to Barton family.